Richardson Publishing Inc.
drkarlenerichardson@aol.com

ISBN-13: 978-0692233894

ISBN-10: 069223389X

Ordering Information:
Quantity sales. Special discounts are available on quantity purchases by corporations, associations, and others. For details, contact the publisher at the email address above.

Bible verses were interpreted from the KJV unless otherwise noted.
Printed in the United States of America

This book is dedicated to my three children
Taisha, Jevon, and Jordan

My granddaughter, Sanaa and son-in-law Delano

My Mother, Mrs. Marie H. Passley
who covers me daily with prayers

This book is dedicated to my three children
Taisha, Jevon, and Jordan

My granddaughter, Sanaa and son-in-law Delano

Gary, My Prayer Partner and Husband

Thank You Lord!

This is possible only because of your patience with me. As I stumbled, falter, and crawled, you remained faithful and never changing.

I love you, I love you, I love you!

A Woman's Take-a-Long Picker-Upper

Only As You

Lord,
I can only be as strong
As your strength in me!
I can only be as wise
As the wisdom your words
give,
I can only be as righteous
As your life I emulate.
Today, I want YOU, be seen
In ME!

Complex

I did not understand life
Until I accepted life as it is.
I did not understand
The power of God
Until I understood
The weaknesses within myself.
I did not understand
The will to survive
Until I understood
That even with intelligence.
I am still not judged by what's
Beneath the color of my skin.

Walk Away

If there is something coming
between you and God.
If there is something coming
between you and inner peace
within your soul.
Walk away and trust God!
Walk away and don't look
back!

God WILL Choose

When you procrastinate
To make a decision,
God always chooses for you.

Instinctively

Always follow your
gut instinct
Especially if your heart is
involved . . .

Solidified!

Thankful for today!
I am so blessed!
I never doubted HIM before
and today solidified that!

HIS Glory!

Sometimes what the enemy
means for bad,
It will actually give
God the Glory!

Take Refuge

(Psalm 34:8)

Blessed is the man

Who takes refuge in HIM.

When trouble comes your way,

Run to the Rock,

Take refuge and be blessed!

My Deliverance

Last night,
I prayed for direction.
Today,
I woke up to my deliverance.
God is an awesome God!

Never

Never take people for granted
Because No matter
How much love is invested
Eventually they get tired!

The Power to Change

The power to change
Lies in the confidence
To make that decision!

Smell The Rose

Take the time
To know your family
Time waits on no one.
I have yet to hear
Of a good employee
At ANYONE'S funeral . . .

Life Goes On

We adapt to new environment
And soon,
Change is no longer noticed!

Can't Quit

I WOULD quit!
But the way
My Jesus is set up . . .

From Gutter To Glory

Stay Calm
I am on my way
From Gutter To Glory!
The next time you see me
You will not recognize
The NEW me!

One Word

There is nothing like being told,
"I am praying for you!"

Trend Setter

In life you have to create your
own opportunities.
Be the trend setter.
The barrier separating you from
your success is confidence.
Without it,
Success is only a dream, and
Your TRUE abilities
Never realized.

Whose Role?

It is not your role to
understand my life . . .
It is my role
To ensure I proceed,
With or without
Your approval.

Ephesians

(Ephesians 6:10-12)

Finally, my brethren,
Be strong in the Lord, and
In the power of his might.
Put on the whole armor
of God, that ye may be able
To stand against the wiles of
the devil!

Why?

Knowing the WHY
Differentiates

Leader vs. Follower

Gone are the days
When a command was followed
Without inquiry.

Steps

Order my steps
Every day Lord!
Else my path becomes crooked
And I go astray,
So please, order my steps
Every day!

Search Me

SEARCH ME please . . .
And know my thoughts,
And Cleanse me
From every sin
And set me free.
Because . . .
You DON'T need to Try me,
Because there ARE
Wicked ways in me . . .

Is it Well?

Each day I must ask
Is it well?
Each day I must refrain
From presumptuously saying,
"It is well"
For each day we wrestle
Not against flesh and blood
So please grant me
Renewed mercies each day
From above!

The Few

Few believed I could or would.
Then I did.
I didn't prove THEM wrong.
I proved me right.
Who has the energy
Trying to prove anyone wrong?

Your Purpose

In life,
You should never
Allow anyone or anything
To deter you
From the course of your purpose.
Know it.
Then Do it.

God's Gift Is YOU

You are different
Because you are special.
There is only ONE like you.
Society may not understand
And that is okay too,
Because the mold broke
The minute God made you!

I Believed

And today,
It was delivered!
I am a witness
To the power of Jesus!

FAITH

If I speak it
I must believe it.
If I believe it
I must conceive it.
If I conceive it
I must birth it.
If I birth it
I must nurture it . . .
Into fruition!

LISTEN:

Never ever underestimate
The Power of PRAYER.
You hear me?
NEVER!!!!

Get Over It!

Okay,

So why are you complaining?

Have you not heard?

Have you not seen?

Have you not known?

Okay, so it didn't work

Okay, so it didn't go as planned!

Get up!

Move on!

Get over it!

Reflection

Many,
Go on the road to Discover
themselves.
But can you face
The man in the mirror?

Already!

Nothing
In life is forever.
Nothing.
So simply get over it!
Already!

Truth

NO ONE or NOTHING
Can validate who you are.
Find the *truth of you* within.

Tomorrow?

When is that?
Who promises that?
Who guarantees a day not yet seen?
You ask: "Is it not by Faith?"
Then where is thy Faith
To complete today
That which should be done today?
And why leave it for tomorrow
That is not promised to any?

A Good Thing

(Romans 8:28)

Know that in ALL things
God works for the good
Of those who love HIM.
So,
What the enemy means for bad
God works for the good!

Steadfast

God is always, always with you
You never doubted before
Don't start now.
Pick up yourself
As in the days of your
beginning
You have come too far
To turn back now!

The Tree

Have I eaten from the tree
Of good and evil?
Am I hiding from Thee?
Yet,
I still hear you
Calling My Name . . .

Making History

It is important!
To treat each day as a day
You make history.
For you.

Inheritance

Capitalize
on
the
inheritance
within.
The Holy Spirit.
It provides the
needed guidance!

Success

Success
Does not come
Simply by wishing
Neither by doing.
Success comes By
The sweat and blood
of your work.

An Art

Glad to have started
To carve out, and
Design my future!
There is hope!

My Investment

The energy I put into making
Someone else's dream come true
I must invest into mine
A hundred fold!

The Bridge

What is the bridge standing between you and your success?

Nobody Greater

The more I feel determined,
The more I know
I HAVE to lean on a power
greater than my own!

Next Leap

It is by FAITH I am taking

my next leap

STILL GOD!

Had a wonderful talk
with God . . .
HE is **STILL GOD!**

Move On!

So you have been:
- hurt?
- deceived?
- betrayed?

At what point do you move away from your past?

Choices

I love the fact
That there are choices
We make them.
We must therefore
bear the consequences.
Choose Right.

My Lord + I!

I am not mysterious
I simply don't reveal my plans
I am not misunderstood
I simply don't feel the need to explain
Because some things
Are just between
Me and my Lord!

Never SEen

Have you ever seen
The righteous forsaken?
Or his seed begging bread?
I therefore rest
On HIS promises
That HE will never leave me
Nor will HE forsake me!

Nobody Greater

People,
May try to break you down
But,
Greater is HE that is in you
Than he that is in the world!

Valleys and Mountains

God,

Only you can see my heart

Its valleys created by deceits

Its mountains built by pain

Heal

Mend

Revive

Bind

Strengthen!

Remove the scars

And then shall it be healed!

In Perspective

Failure ~
The beginning of a
New Adventure
And the End
Of Familiarity

Adaptation

Life doesn't change.

Circumstances do.

Life is constant.

It is We who change

to accommodate the changes

in our circumstances!

Step Aside

I don't feel the need
To oblige your request
Move on
Or better yet
Step out of my way
I have success
To attend to!

Don't Fret

Don't fret
When your path is deterred
Fret
When you stop
Having the vision
To reroute

Get Back Up Again!

Failure
Is not when you have fallen
Failure
Is when you
Refuse to get up!

Delete!

Let the focus of your life
Be on improving the self
If others around
Can't see your vision
Maybe it is time
To press the delete button.

Don't sweat It

Have you smiled
About nothing today?
Have you spent 5 minutes
A L O N E?
Don't take life
So seriously!

Misconception

The biggest misconception is
There always
Has to be a response.
Sometimes
Let your silence speak.

Striking a Balance

Never forget The Lessons in
Your hurt
Your pain
Your scar
Your bruise
It will make you wiser
But try to forget
The who?
The why?
The how?
The where?
Those make you bitter!

No Compromise

I didn't change
Things changed
And I just refused
to compromise!

Just Say No

I've learned
To simply say 'no'
Without the need
To justify
Defend
Explain
Or seek approval!

Live Life

Don't become too ambitious
That you forget to LIVE!

Don't Look Back

To be successful
You have to overcome
The Fear of the unknown
And Step Out on Faith
And then,
Don't look back!
For Nothing!

Who's Rationale?

Never
Try to understand people's
rationale, Unless . . .
It directly impacts Your life!

A Level of Gratitude

In life
Sometimes
No matter how hard you work
It will never be good enough
Stop trying to understand
Other's people's level
Of gratitude!

What IF?

You love HARD
You gave too much
Yet
It still did not work
In retrospect
You would do it all again
Because it is better
To have tried
Than to give up not knowing
The 'What IF'
Or the 'What Could Have Been'

I'm Satisfied!

I only looked back to say
Thank you,
Instead,
I found the scornful look,
And still
I say
Thank you,
For now I know
And can move on
Satisfied!

Now H.E.A.L.E.D.

He played an important role
But I have now healed.
Because of the pain
He inflicted,
I am stronger,
I am wiser,
I am better,
At forgiving!

Walking With Confidence

I am going to walk in
More confidently
I am going to walk in
Claiming my role
I am going to walk in
Knowing that I know
That I am the living proof
Of confidence!

Forgiveness

He cheats
I forgive
He lied
I forgive
He berated
I forgive
When do I love me?

My Destiny

I will say this to me
Each day:
I am beautiful
I am a Queen
I am gifted
I am talented
I am unique
I am who God
Destined me to be!

The WEekend

I choose
Not to care what you think
I choose
Not to care about
Your perspectives
I choose
Not to care about
Your thoughts
I choose
To focus on ME!

Too Busy

You ask me
If I know they gossip?
My response?
No.
I'm too busy doing ME!

Believe

This morning I must believe
This morning I must believe
This morning I must believe
This morning I must believe
This morning I must believe
My very thought
Into existence!

His WoRd

It is HIS word that I am
Resting on
HIS words that provide
Me assurance
HIS words that let me know
Today I am down
But tomorrow
A new dawn awaits me!

My Strength

Don't pity me
Nor offer sympathy
I am not out on my luck
It is just an experience
God has prepared
To strengthen my walk
In HIM!

Stronger

Yesterday I was broken.
Today,
I am stronger,
Much wiser,
All because of my experience
In my brokenness.

Just Call

In your distress
Call on the Lord
HE Will answer!

THaT Call

Yes, they do call
Is it that they are concerned?
Or simply
Want to know what's going on?
Is it empathy?
Or to hear my pain?
Is it friendship?
Or part of
Your gossip chain?
I have nothing to say . . .

As I Rise

I have not deleted you
Not because I am nice
I have not deleted you
Because I need you
To see my rise
As I climb
The stairway of betterment
I need you as a witness
To all
My accomplishments!

Two Sides of a sTory

Stop focusing on
Someone else's version
Of how the story went.
Focus on moving on
From the past instead.

Yesterday

I was asked,
Why do you carry with you
Yesterday?
Today,
I must keep today
Close to my heart.
For yesterday is gone,
And tomorrow not promised.

By FAitH

Because I'm blessed
I can step into
My opportunities by Faith!

HIS Footprints

As I take my next step
On my journey
I still have an ounce of fear.
But by Faith
And Faith alone,
While I may not see
The whole staircase,
But with each stair
I see the imprint
Of HIS footstep ahead,
And I know
He is guiding me!

Wait I Say!

(Jeremiah 29:11)

God declared the plans
HE has for me.
HE declared to prosper me.
HE declared to give me hope.
HE declared to give me a future.
Why then should I not wait
Upon the Lord?

Remain Focus!

(2 Corinthians 4: 16-18)

Though we waste outwardly,

Inwardly we are being renewed.

So we should fix our eyes

Not on what is seen,

But on the unseen.

For only the unseen

Is eternal!

Aim Big!

Stop focusing on small stuff
Set your sights on
Bigger plans.
How great is our God,
That HE would give you
A small portion?

A Reflection of YOU

Surround yourself
With people reflecting
Your vision,
Your purpose,
Your destiny.
Only then
Can you celebrate
With likeminded people!

Within Me

It is important
For me to understand that. . .
I am not always right.
It is okay for me
To not always know
The answer.
And be okay
With those facts.

Because God knows I am not
PERFECT

I am still learning ~

Me.

I am still learning ~

Life.

I am still learning ~

Ways to improve me.

I am still learning ~

Ways to improve my life.

God accepted My learning curve.

Perseverance

(James 1:2-4)

Consider it pure joy
When you are facing trials,
Know that it is necessary
To test your faith.
This develops perseverance,
So you will lack of nothing!

Be Courageous!

(Deuteronomy 32:6)

Be strong!

Be courageous!

Be not afraid!

Be not terrified!

God is with you!

HE will never leave you!

Nor will HE forsake you!

(say this with all the power you have within!)

Stand Firm!

(1 Corinthians 16:13)

Be on your guard.

Always!

Stand firm.

Be one of courage!

Be strong!

Do Not Fear!

(Isaiah 41:10)

Do not fear.

God is with you.

Do not be dismayed.

HE is your God.

HE will strengthen you.

HE will help you.

HE will uphold you.

With HIS righteous

Right Hand!

What a promise!

Walk IN Your Power!

(2 Timothy 1:17)

God did not give you
A spirit of timidity
HE gave you
A spirit of power
HE gave you
A spirit of love
HE gave you
A spirit of self-discipline
Walk in your power!

Sustenance

(Psalm 55:22)

God will NEVER

Let the righteous fall!

Whatever you are going through

Cast your cares on HIM

HE will sustain you!

Do not fight your battle!

It is HIS, and HIS alone!

HE will NEVER

Let the righteous fall!

www.ingramcontent.com/pod-product-compliance
Lightning Source LLC
Chambersburg PA
CBHW021205020426
42331CB00003B/213